The Art Collector's Guide

Buddha's Eye for Beauty

Table of Contents

Chapter 1. Introduction

Immerse yourself in the intoxicating allure of our Special Report: "The Art Collector's Guide: Buddha's Eye for Beauty". Journey with us through the serene pathways of ancient Buddhist art, discovering the heart-stirring spiritual beauty that continues to captivate discerning collectors across the globe. This illuminating report not only introduces you to stunning aesthetics but also the rich historical-cultural context that shaped these sacred artworks. This isn't just a collector's guide; it's your personal key to unlock the metaphorical Buddha's 'Eye for Beauty,' which could truly transform your own vision of art appreciation. With delightful prose and a captivating narrative, we elevate your understanding from casual browsing to insightful collecting. Ready to take the plunge? This special report is not just an investment in your art collection, but in a tradition of timeless beauty!

Chapter 2. Introduction: Buddha's Eye for Beauty

An underlying harmony unifies the universe in its entirety, a harmony that is not readily observable but deeply felt by each one of us. This harmony is not a mere concept, a construction of the mind, it is a pervasive and tangible reality that has profoundly molded the civilizations of humanity since the dawn of consciousness. The understanding of this harmony, and the savoring of its subtle beauty, is the inspiration behind the creation and appreciation of art. And perhaps no culture has captured this essence as vibrantly and thoughtfully as the ancient Buddhist civilizations have done.

The journey through the intricate pathways of ancient Buddhist art is not merely a serene pleasure; it renders profound insights into the rich historical-cultural contexts and the deeply ingrained spiritual ethos that have shaped these art forms. Delving deep into the wellsprings of ancient Buddhist art means embarking on a journey to discover the heart-stirring spiritual beauty that continues to captivate and enlighten discerning art collectors globally, reverberating across the crevices of time and space.

2.1. Understanding the Aesthetic of Serenity

Buddhist art often elicits a sense of calmness and tranquility within its observers. The Buddha's eye for beauty immersed itself in the gentle simplicity of existence – in the rustling leaves, in the purity of a snowflake, in the gentle lapping of waves on an ancient shore. In beholding the art born from such an eye, one enters the realm of the ethereal, brushing against the very essence of existence through the medium of breathtaking visual narratives. A proper exploration of this peaceful aesthetic encourages the observer to enter a mindful trance, letting the essence of the artwork enter their very soul.

This is where the subtlety of the artistic interpretation lies: within the ethereal landscapes and exquisite portraiture, we find the ability to evoke a peace and tranquility that transcends ordinary understanding. It falls upon us to pick apart the layers of these meditative expressions and find the universal truths that they try to convey.

2.2. History and Evolution of Buddhist Art

The roots of Buddhist art run deep, tracing back to the 6th century BCE in the northern Indian subcontinent, where the presence of Buddha was depicted symbolically rather than visually through footprints, bodhi trees, and empty seats. It was not until the 1st century CE that anthromorphic depictions of the Buddha started appearing, particularly in the region of Gandhara.

Through the centuries, as Buddhism journeyed across the vastness of Asia, its art evolved, imbibing the cultural nuances of the regions it blossomed in. This resulted in a myriad of regional styles, each a unique fusion of local sensibilities and traditional Buddhist symbolism. From the strikingly realistic Greco-Bactrian styles of Gandharan art to the intricate celestial beauties of Tantric Buddhist art and the gentle elegance of Japanese Zen art, the stylistic trajectory of Buddhist art is a testament to the adaptability and inclusiveness of Buddhism as a spiritual tradition.

2.3. The Metaphor of Buddha's 'Eye for Beauty'

Buddha's 'Eye for Beauty' is more than just a metaphor; it's a wisdom-infused gaze into the spiritual dimensions of existence and enlightenment. The Buddha's eye looked at the world with profound empathy, kind understanding, and a heightened sense of aesthetics, drawing beauty from even the subtlest aspects of life and existence.

Buddhist art is the symbolic depiction of the Buddha's wisdom, sensibilities, and spiritual enlightenment. By immersing ourselves in the study and appreciation of Buddhist art, we not only unlock the metaphorical Buddha's 'Eye for Beauty,' but also harness its power to transform our own visions of art appreciation.

Buddhist art doesn't just invite us to passively observe; it invites us to understand and thereby participate in the depiction of life, death, and transcendence. It motivates us to adopt a transformative vision, one that can turn the mundane into the extraordinary, the pain into release, the ignorance into enlightenment.

2.4. Shaping your Vision as an Art Collector

In the world of art collection, passion must be coupled with an informed mind. It is essential not only to recognize the outward beauty of a piece but the narrative and history behind it. By stepping into the realm of Buddhist art, you will not only introduce your portfolio to exquisite pieces but to a tradition that has transcended the hands of time.

You are, in essence, collecting the echoes of an ancient spiritual tradition, each resonating differently depending on the symbolism represented or the cultural nuances it incorporates. More than just filling in gaps within your collection, the exploration of Buddhist art may carve a spiritual path, a calming wave of introspection and inspiration that stimulates both your hearts and minds.

The art of collecting is an art in itself, requiring a careful understanding of aesthetic appeal, historical importance, and spiritual significance. Your journey is thus, more than a hunt for artistic treasures; it's an odyssey of pondering, feeling, and resonating with each piece, transforming you into not only a collector of art, but also a connoisseur of mental refinement and spiritual symbolism within the framework of Buddhist art.

As you dive deeper into the profound realms of Buddhist art, realize that the journey is not just about the destination, but also the nuanced cultural landscapes that you traverse, the deep historical contexts that you navigate, and the transformative spiritual insights that you acquire. Remember: each piece you acquire is a statement, a testament to your refined eye for beauty and inherent appreciation for the interconnectedness of art, history, and spirituality.

As we progress course through this comprehensive guide, you will find yourself equipped with the tools to decode the symbolic complexities of Buddhist art, enhancing your appreciation, guiding your curation, and nurturing your vision. With every subsequent chapter, the doors of Buddhist art will swing wider, revealing deeper layers of spiritual beauty and profound wisdom.

Chapter 3. The Roots of Buddhist Art: Origins and Influences

Buddhist Art — a confluence of inspiration, spirituality, culture, and history — traced its roots to ancient times. Originally, Lord Buddha was depicted strictly through symbols; however, the human representation started during the 1st century CE. These transformations, along with many others, have their anchors in various influences, from early Buddhist traditions to varying regional impacts.

3.1. The Early Buddhist Tradition

The Buddhist art tradition began, interestingly, on an aniconic note. Early representations of Buddha did not include human figures; rather, they were mostly symbolic. This practice holds an important place in early Buddhist tradition and was intertwined inherently with its unique philosophies.

Parallel to the teachings of Buddha Shakyamuni, early Buddhist art emphasized the 'anatta' or 'not-self' principle. Buddha was represented through symbols like the Bodhi tree (the tree under which he attained his Enlightenment), footprints, and the Dharmachakra (Wheel of Law). The strict adherence to these symbolic embodiments of the teachings of Buddha was aligned with the fundamental Buddhist principle of non-attachment and impermanence.

Even though the human representations of Buddha were absent, there was a fervent richness in the artistic elements. The Stupas, a significant architectural structure featuring in early Buddhist art, are an example of this. Bountiful in spirit and aesthetics, the Great Stupa at Sanchi, India, manifests detailed narrative reliefs and elaborate gateways that serve as a testament to the artistry of the period.

3.2. Influence of Gandhara and Mathura

The subsequent shift from symbolic to anthropomorphic representations during the 1st century CE stemmed from two primary cultural and artistic centers– Gandhara (modern day Pakistan) and Mathura in northern India. Each region developed its distinctive style, influenced by their historical, cultural, and geographical settings.

In the Gandhara region, the fusion of Indian, Persian, and Greek traditions birthed an idiosyncratic style – the Gandhara School of Art. This gave rise to the Hellenistic-influenced artistic rendition of Buddha, indebted to Greek naturalism and the ideals of physical perfection. The Gandharan Buddhas, made primarily out of gray schist, displayed distinctive Greek-influenced tunics and hairstyles. Furthermore, the adoption of narrative scenes in relief, multi-figured compositions, and spatial depth– all features borrowed from Hellenistic traditions– markedly augmented the storytelling aspect of Buddhist art.

In contrast to the Hellenistic note struck by Gandhara, Mathura styled Buddha based on its indigenous traditions. Mathura art exploited the locally available red sandstone that lent the sculptures their distinctiveness. The Buddhas here were depicted as bare-chested, wrapped in a dhoti, in keeping with the Indian ascetic tradition. The sculptures, both of Buddha and Bodhisattvas, reveal an emphasis on volume, supple body, and taut facial expressions, steering clear of Greek naturalism.

3.3. Influence of Guptas and the Emergence of Mahayana Buddhism

The Gupta period (4th century - 6th century CE) in India, known for classical forms in art, further refined the Mathura style of Buddhist art. The Gupta sculptors crafted the Buddhas with a transcendental serenity and spiritual grace. It's during this period that the features of Buddha, like the lotus-shaped eyes, arched eyebrows, and the 'urna' (the curl of hair in the middle of the forehead representing his divine vision), got stylized and standardized, contributing to the facial tranquility and grace.

Moreover, it's critical to highlight the impact of the emergence of Mahayana Buddhism on Buddhist art. With its focus on the Bodhisattva ideal and the introduction of new Buddhas and Bodhisattvas, Mahayana generated a fresh wave of artistic energy. Avalokiteshvara (the Bodhisattva of compassion), Maitreya (the future Buddha), and Amitabha (Buddha of the West) were new additions who found a place in the Buddhist iconography, enriching the Buddhist art narrative.

3.4. The Silk Road Influence and Expansion to East Asia

The geographical expansion of Buddhism, particularly through the trade routes of the Silk Road, influenced its artistic language profoundly. As Buddhism moved to Central Asia, China, and eventually to Japan and Korea, each region adapted the art to represent their indigenous philosophies and aesthetics.

Buddhism's arrival in China in the 1st century CE launched a new chapter in the chronicle of Buddhist art. The Chinese tradition underscored harmony, hierarchy, and symbolism, impacting the portrayal of the Buddhist scenes and figures. The creation of cave systems like Mogao caves translated Buddhism into a unique blend of architecture, sculpture, and painting.

Similarly, as Buddhism reached Japan and Korea, it gave rise to distinct Buddhist art styles. Japan's Heian period is recognized for the creation of Amida Buddha, and Korea is celebrated for the Seokguram grotto, a testament to the unity of art, religion, and nature.

3.5. Bali and the Southeast Asian Influence

Boasting a rich artistic tradition, the cultural influence of Southeast Asian regions like Thailand, Cambodia, Burma, and Indonesia is perceptible in the evolution of Buddhist art. In Indonesia, the Borobudur temple with its intricate narrative panels showcases stories from Jatakas (Buddha's previous lives) and several stages of Buddhist practice leading towards Enlightenment.

Bali, an Indonesian island predominantly Hindu, also played a role in shaping Buddhist art. The fusion of Hindu and Buddhist elements, inherent in Balinese culture, carved an exclusive style – syncing seamlessly with the spiritual vibe of the island.

In conclusion, the trajectory of Buddhist art reflects a melange of influences, invigorated by the territories it traversed. Over centuries it absorbed elements from different cultures, while maintaining its distinct philosophical core. From symbols inspired by the Buddha's life and teachings to representations influenced by the Hellenistic and indigenous styles, from the refined grace of the Gupta period to the culturally-dynamic East Asian impressions– the Buddhist art history whirls in a dance of constant evolution, yet remaining austerely persistent in embodying its spiritual essence. Now, as discerning collectors, you are not merely appreciating the art for its visual grandeur, but you're venerating an artistic tradition sculpted through a rich historical and cultural chronicle.

Chapter 4. Representations of Buddhahood: Depicting the Divine

A deep, spiritual desire for self-realization fuelled the creation of divine representations in ancient Buddhist art. These artworks, profound in their aesthetic and philosophical appeal, visually articulate the sacred journey and nature of the Buddha, serving as an extraordinarily nuanced mirror reflecting the paths to enlightenment.

4.1. The Turbulent Origins

Buddha portraits emerge not from cultural vacuity but rise with the tide of adversity during the period of formational Buddhism. After Buddha's death—his parinirvana—there were hesitations to delineize his physical semblance directly, attributing to the fear it might reduce the profound philosophy and teachings to mere human individuality. Instead, the early Aniconic Period, approximately 5th century BC – 1st century AD, bore essential symbolic representations. In place of the humanized Buddha, symbols such as Empty Thrones, Bodhi Trees, Stupas (niches), Footprints, and Dharma Wheels spoke volumes about the enigmatic teachings and way of life preached by Buddha.

However, as Buddhism reached the interiors of Gandhara (modern-day Pakistan and Afghanistan) through Silk Road, an inevitable cultural and artistic amalgamation gave rise to the practice of direct anthropomorphic representations. Fuelled by the Hellenistic influences, especially the precision and grace perfected by ancient Greek sculptors, the 1st century began what was known as the Gandharan Buddhist Art. It saw the creation of Buddha's physical representations, making him a visible entity that resonated with followers on a new level. It was the dawn of the Gandharan Buddhas, impeccably combining Indian symbolism with nuanced Greco-Roman detailed human anatomy.

4.2. The Transcendental Bodies

Buddhist philosophy articulates the existence of three bodies (tri-kaya) of Buddha - the Nirmanakaya, Sambhogakaya, and Dharmakaya. The Nirmanakaya, or transformational bodies, are earthly incarnations of Buddha that have experienced birth and death. The Sambhogakaya, or bliss bodies, exist in a liminal space between the form and the formless, crystallizing the epiphanies Buddha experienced. However, the Dharmakaya, or truth body, exists beyond the tangible or intangible realms, making it elusive for artistic depiction.

The Nirmanakaya were the first to be sculpted, given the more relatable human form. The Gandharan Buddhas, created out of gray schist, managed to capture the meditative calm, wise eyes, and flowing garments with an uncanny finesse, making visible the spiritual Buddha to the mortal world. With the Sambhogakaya, seen primarily in Tibetan Thangkas, artists ventured into surreal landscapes. They showcased the celestial Buddhas and Boddhisatvas amidst paradisiacal settings, epitomizing spiritual opulence.

Nevertheless, the elusive Dharmakaya was often represented indirectly by a luminous orb, an empty throne, or the infinite emptiness, underscoring the formlessness of the universal truth he symbolizes.

4.3. Iconography of Mudras and Symbols

The power of Buddha representations extended beyond the mere physical. Mudras, symbolic hand gestures, play vital roles in communicating spiritual messages. The earliest Dharmachakra Mudra, representing the first sermon in Deer Park, or the persuasive Bhumisparsha Mudra, symbolizing the call to Earth to witness Buddha's supreme enlightenment, convey profound philosophical tenets through simple gestures.

Buddha's iconic features such as the Urna (a curl between eyebrows), Ushnisha (protuberance on the head), elongated ears, lotus positions, and the presence of animals and trees, further enrich the narrative, symbolizing the transformative journey from a royal prince to an enlightened being.

4.4. The Journey Towards Abstraction

As Mahayana Buddhism spread across Asia, the representation of the divine evolved. In the robust figures of China's Tang dynasty, the spiritual Buddha becomes a celestial Buddha. Korean Buddhist sculptors carved more serene expressions, instilling a profound peace. Japanese Esoteric sects fashioned wrathful deities who protected the Buddhist doctrine.

In contrast, the growing impact of meditation (Zen) in Japan saw the gradual abstraction in portraits. These minimalist ink paintings, void of ornate details, encapsulated the essence of Buddha, echoing with the Zen belief in simplicity and meditation.

Fascinatingly, the artistry of Buddhist sculptures and paintings continues to evolve, embodying cultural particularities while holding on to the foundational Buddhist philosophies. It is astounding how such cumulative creative expression concentrates on so many fine details and still encapsulates a vast universe of spiritual ideology.

Chapter 5. Timelines and Traditions: Evolution of Buddhist Art Across Cultures

The genesis of Buddhist art can't be traced back to a single origin or timeline. Its evolution is intriguingly interwoven with the path Buddhism itself has taken over centuries. Spanning across multiple civilizations, adapting to the local culture and aesthetics, this art form thrived, making an indelible imprint on each region's artistic heritage.

5.1. Spring of Buddhist Art: India (5th Century BCE - 12th Century CE)

Any exploration of the evolution of Buddhist aesthetics would be incomplete without addressing its birthplace: India. Following the death of Gautama Buddha around 5th century BCE, his teachings spread widely, evoking a profound artistic response. The earliest expressions of Buddhist art in India were aniconic, using symbols such as the Bodhi tree, the lotus, the dharma wheel, and the Buddha's footprints, rather than direct depictions of the Buddha himself.

However, by the 1st century CE, concurrent with the rise of the Gandhara and Mathura schools of art, this convention gave way to anthropomorphic representations of the Buddha. The grand sculptures of the Buddha produced during this era, accentuated by Greek-inspired realism and Indian symbolism, continue to mesmerize art connoisseurs today.

5.2. Tracing the Silk Route: Central Asia (1st Century BCE - 10th Century CE)

Next, journey along the Silk Road, where the remarkable Greco-Buddhist art form was born. This style synthesizes the realistic human imagery of Greek art with Buddhist iconography, most notably in the region of Gandhara, setting the stage for what's to come in Central Asian Buddhist art. The amalgamation of various cultures resulted in vibrant frescoes, exquisite sculptures, and intricate decorative arts, reflecting philosophical depth and the sublime aesthetics of Buddhism.

5.3. The Land of the Rising Sun: Japan (6th Century - Present)

Buddhist art entered Japan in the 6th century through Korea and China during the Asuka and Nara periods. The Japanese embraced Buddhism and its resonating aesthetics, adorning their temples with stone and wooden sculptures depicting the Buddha and Bodhisattvas. Each subsequent dynasty developed its own artistic identity, from the realism of the Heian period to the abstract interpretations during the Kamakura period, profoundly impacting the country's cultural fabric.

5.4. Dragon's Embrace: China (1st Century - Present)

From the 1st century CE, Buddhist art started to influence Chinese culture, a relationship that persisted intensity for centuries. Adapting to local aesthetics and traditions, it resulted in a unique fusion distinctive to Chinese Buddhist art. Intricate bronze iconography, monumental cave temples adorned with sculptures and murals like those at Dunhuang, colossal stone Buddhas in Longmen and Yungang bear testament to Buddhism's lasting influence in China.

5.5. Lotus Blooms: Southeast Asia (1st Century - Present)

In South Asia, especially in the regions now known as Myanmar, Thailand, Laos, and Cambodia, Buddhism arrived early on. And with it, came Buddhist art. Manifesting the beliefs and philosophies of Buddhism, local artists created sculptures, murals, and architectures. From the grandeur of the Borobudur in Indonesia, the Angkor Wat in Cambodia, to the harmonious fusion of indigenous and Buddhist motifs in Thai artwork, Southeast Asia houses a rich repository of unique, culturally significant Buddhist masterpieces.

5.6. Blending with Shamanism: Korea (4th Century - 20th Century)

Korean Buddhist art emerged in the fourth century CE, bearing influence from Chinese and Central Asian styles. Yet, with the infusion of local shamanistic rituals and beliefs, it managed to develop a unique character. A noteworthy development in Korean Buddhist art is the production of gilt-bronze sculptures during the Three Kingdoms Period, which are considered pivotal both in terms of aesthetics and craftsmanship.

5.7. Mystic Universe of Tibet (7th Century - Present)

Fiercely guarding its isolation, Tibet's encounter with Buddhism in the 7th century paved the way for a radical transformation in its art.

The distinctive Thangka paintings - intricate, spiritual representations typically on cotton or silk appliqué, hand-painted scroll paintings, mandalas, statues, and sand arts - these Tibetan art forms have become the torchbearers of the Vajrayana tradition of Buddhism, mesmeric and spiritually uplifting.

In summation, the evolution of Buddhist art across cultures manifests an enthralling journey, revealing how each civilization, while sharing a common philosophical foundation, shaped its distinct artistic vocabulary. Every region, while embracing the profound ethos of Buddhism, colored it with their cultural palette, creating a diverse, yet unified pageantry of aesthetics – a true testament to the Buddhist vision of oneness in diversity.

Chapter 6. Recognizing Symbols: Decoding Buddhist Iconography

In the vast universe of Buddhist artwork, symbolism permeates every line, shape, and color. Recognizing these symbols and deciphering their meanings is critical to appreciating the narratives woven into this sacred art. Not just that, it might offer a lens into the Buddha's 'Eye for Beauty'. As art collectors, it is the awareness of iconography that elevates our understanding from casual browsing to insightful collecting.

6.1. The Auspicious Eight

Perhaps the most widespread symbols in Buddhist iconography are the Astamangala, or the 'Auspicious Eight'. These eight symbols originated in ancient Indian iconography before being adopted by different cultures of East, Tibetan and Theravada Buddhism, and varying slightly based on cultural context.

- The Endless Knot: Represents the interconnected nature of reality, where everything is interlinked with everything else.

- The Lotus Flower: This symbolizes purity and enlightenment. A lotus flower grows in muddy water, yet remains unstained, an analogy for a person's spiritual journey.

- The Dharmachakra: The Wheel of Dharma represents the Buddha's teachings, its eight spokes symbolizing the Noble Eightfold Path.

- The Victory Banner: The Dhvaja or Victory Banner is a symbol of Buddha's victory over the impediments on the path to enlightenment.

- The Golden Fishes: Seen in pairs, the fishes symbolize happiness and freedom.

- The Treasure Vase: Known as the Kalasha, this represents spiritual and material abundance.

- The Parasol: The Chattra or the Parasol is a symbol of protection and shelter from all harm.

- The Conch Shell: The Shankha represents the teachings and wisdom of the Buddha, resonating across the universe.

6.2. Manifestations of Buddha

In many artworks, Buddha doesn't always appear in human form. Instead, through a range of bodhisattvas and deities, the Buddha's teachings and aspects are often represented in different physical forms.

- Avalokiteśvara or Guanyin: As the Bodhisattva of Compassion, Avalokiteshvara can appear in many forms. In Chinese Buddhism, Avalokiteshvara is known as Guanyin and is portrayed as a female figure.

- Manjushri: The Bodhisattva of Wisdom, Manjushri, is usually depicted holding a flaming sword in his right hand, representing the power of wisdom, and a lotus flower or book in his left.

- Tara: The female Bodhisattva or Goddess, Tara is an important figure in Tibetan Buddhism. She symbolizes compassion, helps in overcoming fear and obstacles, and mostly appears in two forms– Green Tara and White Tara.

- Amoghasiddhi: One of the Five Buddha Families in Buddhism, Amoghasiddhi is often portrayed with a fearless gesture and holds a double vajra.

6.3. The Six Perfections

One key aspect of Buddhist philosophy is the Paramitas or The Six Perfections. Buddhist artwork communicates these concepts through various means, often employing symbolic elements.

- Generosity (Dana): Often depicted as open palms, a tree bearing fruit, or a pot pouring water, all symbolizing the act of giving.

- Morality (Sila): This is emphasized via symbols like an elephant - representing mental calm and restraint over passions, or a bowl - representing renunciation.

- Patience (Kshanti): Illustrated by trees and plants, signifying endurance and resistance to harsh conditions.

- Vigor (Virya): Represented by a lion or a horse, popular symbols for strength and effort.

- Meditation (Dhyana): Indicated by a meditating figure, showing serenity and concentration.

- Wisdom (Prajna): Often conceived as a flame or torch, conveying illumination of darkness or ignorance.

6.4. Colors in Buddhist Art

Interpreting color symbolism is another substantial aspect of decoding Buddhist art. Five colors often dominate Buddhist art: white, yellow, red, blue, and green.

- White: Represents purity and liberation.

- Yellow: Often seen in monks' robes, this color represents humility and renunciation.

- Red: Symbolizes subjugation and power.

- Blue: Blue like the sky or the ocean is a symbol for infinity and depth.

- Green: It signifies balance, harmony, and vigor.

Understanding these symbols will help any art collector gain a deeper appreciation of the intricate layers of meaning packed into Buddhist artwork. As you traverse the quiet halls of art galleries and exhibitions, take a moment to recognize these symbols and reflect on what the artist was trying to convey. With each artwork, remember that you are not just investing in an item, but a tradition of timeless beauty.

Chapter 7. Major Buddhist Art Forms: A Deep Dive into Statuary and Thangkas

Immersed in a sublime world of intricate symbolism and profound spirituality, we initiate our journey in the realm of two seminal Buddhist Art forms: Statuary and Thangkas. Exploring these distinguished art forms is akin to embarking on a spiritual soujourn, where every detail is a testament to the enlightened path the Buddha paved for humanity.

7.1. The Buddha Statues: Paragons of Serenity

It is believed that the semblance of the Buddha is not just an imprint of his physical features but a projection of his enlightened spirit. Buddha statues vary in styles, materials, and posing gestures, known as Mudras, across different Buddhist traditions.

The earliest Buddha statues, known as aniconic images, did not depict the physical form of the Buddha but symbolized his teachings and life events. It wasn't until the reign of the Kushan king Kaniska, in the 1st-2nd centuries AD, that anthropomorphic representations of the Buddha emerged in the wider Gandharan and Mathuran art styles.

Gandhara, reflecting Greco-Roman influences, produced statues often made from gray schist or stucco, exhibiting a realistic and detailed representation of the Buddha. Meanwhile, Mathura, utilizing red sandstone, exuded a more indigenous, abstract, and robust craftsmanship.

Abundant in symbolism, the statues itself and the various attributes associated with them convey profound spiritual messages. For instance, the Mudras signify various life events and virtues of the Buddha, associating with his enlightened mission.

For instance, in the 'Dharmachakra Mudra,' the Buddha's hands gesture the turning of the Dharma wheel, symbolizing his first sermon in Sarnath. Meanwhile, the 'Bhumisparsha Mudra' image showcases Buddha calling the Earth as a witness to his enlightenment.

7.2. Thangkas: Sacred Scrolls of Wisdom

The Tibetan Thangka, translating to "recorded message," serves as devotional artefact, visual aid for monastic education, and a meditation tool. Essentially, a Thangka is a painted or embroidered Buddhist banner itinerant monks would carry from village to village.

What makes Thangkas unique is their overt emphasis on evoking the spiritual dimension. Each painting, meticulously crafted, serves as a window into the exalted realms of the Buddhas, Bodhisattvas, deities, and mandalas.

Crafting a Thangka is considered a meditative practice. Each line, each brushstroke is imbued with a sense of mindful tranquility, blurring the boundaries between the artisan and the divine.

In terms of structure, Thangkas deploy complex iconography. Buddhas or Bodhisattvas are usually in the center, surrounded by lesser figures, scenes, and elaborate geometric designs.

A special mention must be made about Mandala thangkas. Mandalas, meaning 'circle' in Sanskrit, are symbolic representations of the Buddhist Universe. A Mandala Thangka, displayed during significant ceremonies or used during meditation, serve as a blueprint of the divine abode of the deity it illustrates.

7.3. From Sacred to Collection: Procuring Art with Respect

Irrespective of their form, Buddhist artworks convey messages of compassion, wisdom, and mindfulness. Therefore, as a collector, it is essential not just to appreciate their aesthetic charm but also respect their spiritual significance. Reputed art dealers can offer practical advice, ensuring your acquisitions are legally and ethically sourced.

Whether be it statues or Thangkas, understanding and appreciating Buddhist art is a rewarding endeavor – much like spotting an oasis of calm amidst the chaotic whirl of life. Through these exquisite art forms, we do not merely perceive the beauty they represent, we partake in a spiritual narrative that stimulates our hearts into experiencing a profound serenity, a Zen-like state. Prompted by the Buddha's eye for beauty, we approach art not just with our logical faculties but infuse our entire being into the gratifying process of art-appreciation.

Chapter 8. The Importance of Provenance: Deciphering Artistic Authenticity

The scent of history clings to every tangible piece of art. As an ardent appreciator or a discerning collector, the ability to recognize this historical aroma, often known as provenance, is crucial in the world of art collection. Provenance is the chronicle of ownership, a veritable detective's diary that traces artwork from its origin to the present day. It is a narrative that encompasses not just the biography of a physical entity-- the artwork-- but also the history it has witnessed and participated in through times of peace or violence, prosperity or destitution, creation or destruction. Recognizing an artwork's provenance is like holding a piece of history in your hands.

8.1. Understanding the Scope of Provenance

Art collectors and curators understand that the value of an artwork is not just invested in the aesthetics or the name of the artist. True value lies in the artwork's journey, its lineage, the history it has accrued over time. The provenance, a term derived from the French word 'provenir' meaning to come from, encapsulates this journey, and bears witness to the life of an artwork.

From origins in the artist's studio to ownership by art dealers, galleries, and private collectors, each instance when the artwork changes hands creates a part of its provenance. Additionally, the artwork's exhibition history, where it has been exhibited, and acknowledgement in professional catalogues or other scholarly works all contribute to its provenance. It's an ongoing dialogue between the creation and the created.

8.2. Significance of Provenance in Buddhist Art

In the specific context of Buddhist art, provenance becomes even more important. Buddhist art traces its origins back to ancient civilizations, and hence holds witness to centuries of evolution and transformation. This traces a route that passes through the hands of the artist who first breathed life into the image, to its role as an object of worship, a war prize, a bulk trade item, or coveted collector's piece, each chapter adding to its richness.

Artworks, such as Buddha statues, reliefs and Thangka paintings, once served distinctly spiritual purposes. They were created as a medium to spread Buddhist teachings or to inspire devotion, rather than merely decorative items or collectibles. Since these artworks contain spiritual significance steeped in symbolism and iconography, understanding their provenance is critical.

8.3. Provenance as the Key to Authenticity

In the realm of art collection, provenance can serve as a warranty of authenticity. For each work of art, determining the authenticity is just as important as appreciating the aesthetics. Unraveling provenance is similar to peeling an onion - it discloses layers of information about the artwork's history, its owners, and potential restorations or alterations it might have undergone.

Provenance can verify an artwork's authenticity, ensuring protection against forgeries or replicas. Most importantly, accurate, documented provenance can significantly increase the artwork's value. However, it's easier said than done. Provenance research demands extensive knowledge, meticulous investigation, and sometimes good luck.

8.4. Challenges in Provenance Research

As enchanting as the pursuit of provenance can be, it is far from effortless. Each artwork's journey is interconnected with a larger narrative; layers of historical, politico-social, and economic contexts. In the backdrop of looted artefacts, illegal smuggling, and instances of cultural colonization, reconstructing an artwork's provenance can raise contentious issues and ethical debates.

Incomplete records, non-standardized documentation, or missing links in the chain of ownership are common hurdles that cast a cloud of uncertainty. These complications amplify when discussing antiquities, like ancient Buddhist art, where the passage of time may have eroded key pieces of information. Therefore, provenance research is a relentless quest that demands perseverance and tenacity.

8.5. Deciphering Artistic Authenticity: A Conclusion

Provenance is undoubtedly one of the ultimate keys to unlock 'Buddha's Eye for Beauty'. It is an exploration, a search for truth, a pursuit of the artwork's soul. Understanding an artwork's provenance allows you to know the artwork beyond its physicality, to understand its spirit, its journey, and its voice.

Whether you're drawn towards the serene faces of Gandhara Buddha statues or the ethereal charm of Tibetan Thangkas, understanding their provenance will not only enrich your art-collecting experience but elevate your understanding to new heights. Remember: each artwork has a story to tell, and provenance is the language that articulates this tale; your fine-tuned understanding of this language has the potential to truly transform your vision of art appreciation.

As you traverse through the captivating landscape of Buddhist art, bear in mind that the provenance isn't just about the artists, the periods, or the regions—it's about connecting with the life of the artwork itself, and becoming a part of its continuing story. Remember, you're not just an art collector, you're a custodian of these living vestiges of history.

Chapter 9. Building a Collection: Practical Guide for Budding Collectors

Budding collectors often face the daunting task of crafting a personalized collection from scratch. Embarking on this journey requires not only an appreciation for Buddhist art but also a discerning eye and understanding of the historical and cultural significance of the pieces. Here's a comprehensive guide to help you chart your course.

9.1. Assessing Your Interests and Understanding Your Motivations

Art collection is an intensely personal endeavor with motivations varying widely among collectors. Sow the seeds of your collection by first understanding your reasons for venturing into the world of Buddhist art. Do you feel a deep spiritual connection to the artistic depictions of Buddha? Are you engaged by the historical narratives associated with the various Buddhist dynasties and their unique artistic expressions? Or is it purely an aesthetic interest that draws you? Recognizing your pull can help shape a cohesive collection that best reflects your personality and passion.

9.2. Educating Yourself

Immersion is key to gaining a deep understanding of this realm. Read books, attend seminars, participate in online communities, and consult with experts. A strong understanding of Buddhist art's cultural and historical context enriches your appreciation and fuels more informed collecting.

Essential subjects cover the diverse range of Buddhist art forms across the different cultures, the various materials used, and the significance of recurring motifs. You should also study the art market and familiarize yourself with the trends, the pivotal artists, auction performances, and price points.

9.3. Setting a Budget

Art can be an expensive investment, and costs can quickly escalate. Set a realistic budget considering not only the acquisition cost but also costs associated with insurance, maintenance, possible restoration, and storage. Being financially prepared helps avoid buyer's remorse and debt.

9.4. Where to Buy

Acquiring Buddhist art can happen through several channels. Auction houses, art galleries, and international art fairs are popular options. Online platforms have also made it possible to buy authenticated art from reputed dealers around the world.

Each channel offers its own benefits. Auction houses can provide opportunities to grab pieces at competitive prices, while galleries offer a curated collection of works. Online platforms offer convenience and a wide selection but require a degree of caution regarding authenticity.

9.5. Vet the Authenticity and Provenance

The value of a piece lies in its authenticity, age, and provenance, making these vital factors when considering a purchase. Demand a certificate of authenticity and a provenance report, especially for ancient art. High-quality fakes or replicas are rampant in the market and distinguishing them from genuine articles can be challenging, even for experienced buyers.

Engage with reputed art consultants, restorers, or academic experts to establish the authenticity. Securing pieces with a well-documented history and lawful ownership details will eventually increase the value and marketability of your collection.

9.6. Caring for Your Collection

Proper maintenance is crucial to preserve your collection's integrity. Different materials require varying care. For instance, bronzes need controlled humidity, paints need protection from light, and textiles need to be kept free of dust and insects.

Your art deserves a safe and comfortable home. Arrange your pieces to complement each other and enhance your living space. Consider professional framing for delicate artworks and installing secure display systems for heavier ones. Adequate insurance for your collection is also highly recommended.

9.7. Enjoy the Journey

Collecting art is not just about acquiring objects but embarking on a fulfilling personal journey. The excitement of exploring art forms, the anticipation of the next acquisition, the joy of sharing your collection with others, and the pride of owning a piece of history make the process an enriching experience.

Remember, a collection is never truly complete. There is always a new piece to discover, a new historical significance to unearth, or a new artistic style to appreciate. Let the constant pursuit of knowledge and beauty guide your journey in this world of Buddhist art.

Chapter 10. Preserving Buddhist Art: Conservation and Care

Buddhist art, with its intricate designs and spiritual symbolism, is more than just a visual spectacle. It is a tangible link to our past, a celebration of our shared human culture and spirituality. As such, the preservation of these invaluable pieces of art is a task of utmost importance. Your role as a collector involves not only acquiring and appreciating the artwork but also maintaining its physical integrity and prolonged survival.

10.1. Understanding the Materials and Techniques

Buddhist art has been created over several centuries using a variety of mediums and materials, including but not limited to stone, wood, metal, ceramics, and textiles. Each material has its own unique characteristics, and understanding these is crucial to their preservation.

Stone sculptures can last for thousands of years if properly maintained and protected from the elements. They are resilient but can be susceptible to erosion, particularly from wind and rain. They can also be affected by biological growth, such as lichen, which can slowly eat away at the stone.

Wood, used extensively in temple structures and sculptures, needs to be protected from damage by insects and decay from moisture. It also requires a stable environment to prevent cracking due to fluctuations in temperature and humidity.

Metals, such as bronze and gold, need to be polished to guard against tarnishing. They are susceptible to corrosion, and high levels of humidity can accelerate this process.

Ceramic pieces are sturdy, but they are also brittle and can easily break if not handled carefully. Like any glazed artwork, ceramics are sensitive to light, which can cause the colors to fade over time.

Textiles, used for temple banners and ritual costumes, are often sensitive to light, heat, and moisture. They need to be stored carefully to prevent deterioration, and methods such as vacuum-freeze-drying might be employed if necessary.

Likewise, materials such as thangkas — painted or embroidered Buddhist banner which was traditionally kept unframed and rolled up when not on display — call for careful regular dusting and protection from light, moisture, and pests.

Understanding the materials and techniques used in producing a piece of Buddhist art helps determine the ideal conditions for its preservation and display, and identify when professional conservation may be needed.

10.2. Display and Storage Conditions

Providing the right environmental conditions can do much to slow the rate of decay and keep the artwork in a good state for longer. Light, temperature, and humidity play vital roles, making them key elements that every art collector and curator ought to consider.

Most materials used in Buddhist art are sensitive to light — particularly direct sunlight and fluorescent light, which emit high levels of ultraviolet radiation. Reducing light levels, controlling the amount of daylight entering the room, and investing in UV filters can help mitigate this risk.

Temperature and humidity also play a critical role in preservation. Fluctuations in temperature can lead to the physical expansion and contraction of materials, which over time may result in damage. Similarly, high humidity levels can increase the risk of biological growth and salt efflorescence, especially in stone and wooden sculptures.

The ideal temperature for storage and display should, however, depend on the materials of the artwork. Totems carved from wood, for instance, can be stored at a temperature of around 20°C. It is generally recommended to maintain the relative humidity between 40% and 60% to prevent dryness or dampness.

10.3. Practical Steps to Cleaning and Maintenance

Regular cleaning can prolong the life of an artwork. Dust and dirt accumulation can lead to damage and can harbor pests that could cause further harm.

Generally, it is recommended to dust the pieces using a soft brush. Avoid using cleaning products on the surface unless you've consulted with a conservation professional. Should there be any stubborn dirt, it's better not to push ahead with aggressive cleaning methods. Instead, contact a professional conservator as they possess the knowledge and skills needed for safe and effective cleaning.

In some instances, such as with ancient stone sculptures, it may become necessary to control and remove biological growth. Again, this should be left to professionals as the incorrect application of biocides can potentially lead to more harm than good.

10.4. When and How to Seek Professional Help

Care and preservation of Buddhist art, particularly ancient pieces of high value, should not be without the guidance of a professional conservator. It's good practice to have an established relationship with a conservator who can provide both advice and practical assistance when needed.

Professional conservators can help create a suitable environment for your artwork in terms of lighting, temperature, and humidity. They can guide you on the best procedures for cleaning your artwork and provide you with a detailed condition report.

If a piece becomes damaged, professional conservation treatment can help recover lost integrity and aesthetics. It's important not to undertake any restoration work without professional help, as improper methods can lead to irreparable harm and significant loss of value.

10.5. Proper Documentation and Records

One essential aspect of preserving Buddhist art is keeping thorough records. Good documentation includes photographs and descriptions of the initial condition of the artwork, details of any professional conservation work done, and those of the display or storage environment.

Detailed records are not only useful for tracking changes in the condition of a piece but also for insurance purposes. In addition, should the artwork ever need to be sold, having extensive documentation can enhance its provenance and potentially its value.

Collecting and preserving Buddhist art is about more than owning beautiful objects. It's about safeguarding a sacred heritage. As stewards of this valuable legacy, collectors have a critical role to play in maintaining the integrity of this art form and ensuring it can be enjoyed by future generations. So embrace this role with respect, knowledge, and the proper care it requires.

Through careful consideration, diligent care, and a close working relationship with professionals in conservation, you can not only enjoy your collection but also pass on these pristine testaments of history and spirituality to future generations.

Chapter 11. Conclusion: The Enduring Allure of Buddhist Art

Our journey through the serene, spiritual, and fascinating world of Buddhist art is nearing its end. It has been a revealing journey, highlighting the importance of understanding the context and culture of these profound and awe-inspiring creations. The road taken has been a spiritual and artistic pilgrimage. Now we stand at its culmination, the concluding chapter, where together, we'll wrap up our exploration and ponder over the enduring allure of Buddhist art.

Treading through the magic of Buddhist art, we perceived the intricate tapestry of symbolism, the deep-rooted lessons inherent in each artwork. More than just objects to be admired, each artifact holds within its folds the very spirit of Buddhism – the relinquishment of desire, pursuit of spiritual awakening, and harboring compassion for all. Art, here, is not bound by the ephemeral physicality; it is imbued with timeless philosophies which continuously radiate with the vibrancy of the Buddha's teachings.

11.1. The Paradox of Buddhist Art Advancement

Buddhist art has evolved and flourished over the centuries, casting its influence across diverse cultures and geographical landscapes. Each transformation, each involvement with new cultures, didn't falsify its preliminary essence; rather it morphed, shaped itself to narrate the tale of Buddha's teachings through fresh lenses. It's a paradox worth exploring - how Buddhist art wrapped itself around local art traditions while maintaining its core values and ideas.

This ability to synthesize elements of contrasting cultures while upholding original teachings is undoubtedly one of the reasons why Buddhist art resonates so strongly. It stands as a global unifier, a beacon of connectivity among different civilizations throughout history. The multifaceted journey of Buddhist art is a testament to its enduring allure, intrinsically encompassing the Buddha's teachings in adapting and harmonising with the world.

11.2. The Timeless Value of Buddhist Art

In a fast-paced, often materialistic world, the calming tranquillity that Buddhist art imbues offers solace. In moments of quiet communication with the aesthetically fascinating objects, one discerns not only the historical-cultural context but engages in introspection and spiritual exploration. Each artefact, each mural weaves a narrative of Buddhist teachings, which ensnare the collectors with their profound, timeless wisdom.

Whether it's appreciating the artistic beauty of a Thangka painting, or meditating on the tranquil gaze of a Buddha statue, one may feel the undercurrent of peace inherent in Buddhist philosophy. Perhaps, that's the reason why Buddhist art, even in this modern age, summons a strong pull. Its relevance and resonance are not bound by time, but rather, they persist, reminding us of the unwavering pertinence of Buddha's lessons in our lives.

11.3. The Art Collector's Perspective: Enlightening the 'Eye for Beauty'

Possessing a piece of Buddhist art extends beyond the traditional practice of art collection. It's akin to inheriting a piece of history, of philosophy, of timeless teachings. It isn't merely about the monetary investment but the spiritual enlightening accompanying it. Every artifact, sculpture, painting, or architecture, is a story that encapsulates age-old wisdom, cradling the potential to uplift your understanding and appreciation of art and existence.

Recognizing this essence and being able to tap into the deep spiritual reservoir that each piece of Buddhist Art encapsulates requires the metaphorical Buddha's 'Eye for Beauty.' This intuition combines aesthetic appreciation with an insightful interpretation of accompanying symbolism, taking you further on the spiritual-artistic journey.

11.4. Toward a Greater Understanding

The exploration of Buddhist art opens a window to parallel realms of spirituality and artistry. The path leads toward a greater understanding, an enriched perception. In the process, one's eyes are opened to the beauty not only contained within physical manifestations but also the ethereal aura they imbibe.

The profound journey through the historic-cultural pathway of Buddhist art ends here, though the insights gleaned continue to impact. As we leave this artistic pilgrimage, we carry with us a renewed outlook. The experience calls for introspection, urging us to cherish, to explore more and to immerse further, becoming not just collectors of artwork but inheritors of timeless serenity.

Buddhism's intrinsic values - compassion, mindfulness, and spiritual awakening - resonate across centuries, telling a tale not just of an ancient religion, but of an enduring philosophy. It's hardly surprising then that the artwork born from these teachings continues to captivate, fascinates, and enriches collectors across the world. Buddhist art, with its eternal allure, does not merely face history; it carries it forward, keeping alive the teachings of the Buddha in all their glory.

As art collectors and appreciators of Buddhist art, we stand with one foot in the past and one in the present, acting as conduits for these precious artifacts and their inherent wisdom, helping to guide them into the future. Through our pursuit of art, we become part of an enduring story, preserving and promoting not just artifacts but a philosophy of compassion and enlightenment for subsequent generations. Thus, the allure of Buddhist art endures, its spiritual and aesthetic beauty continues to intrigue, captivate and inspire, a timeless testament to the teachings of Buddha.